Sometimes, I have a heart

Sometimes, I have a heart

BY K.G. GINLEY

Supervising Editors: Caitlin Chrismon, Emily Oliver
Associate Editors: Taylor Munsell, Viviana Moreno
Internal Formatting: Viviana Moreno
Cover Designer: Emily Cyr

GenZPublishing.org
Aberdeen, NJ

To everyone who ever broke my heart— You weren't very kind, but you did inspire art.

And, of course, to my family and friend— Without you, I'd never believe love could make amends

Virginia, My Love

Sometimes I catch myself writing about your existence—
in the stars,
in the world,
but most importantly, in my heart.

And I can't help but let a wave of sentiment wash over me,
drowning me,
taking me under your charm even further.
I do not know if it was a storm or an iceberg, but my vision has been stolen from me, and I am sinking into cold waters, aligning myself with sunken ships and skeletons that never had the privilege and curse of seeing you. But I find myself on the bottom of the ocean— violent waves of emotion that were too strong to sail upon the surface of your skin.

Do you even realize what you've done? That you've cost me the chance to survive?

There's blood in the water, and I hope it's you circling me, but the teeth are too sharp and your current touch is Pacific, but my grave is in the Atlantic, right next to the overturned lifeboat you forgot to cut loose. *Forgot.*

It is my greatest folly and my greatest act of courage that I believed the song you sang, the poems you whispered into my ears, the vision you painted on the canvas of my mind with the red and pink hues of the sunset—
But you placed a gilded frame that cut off the hellfire in the form of a blue abyss from my sight.
I was burned by a force of nature that should have pushed me to the shores of sanity, and what does that say about me?

Instead, a siren's sigh prevented the animal in me from
running from the edge I created—
"Escape is futile."
There's a boney grip on my wrists from the remains of fools
like me, and whatever is out there is coming closer—
At least the sight from below the universe is almost as
tragically beautiful as us.

Ember Eyes

Her eyes were not blue like the sky but like the hottest flames of a fire.
Mistakenly bright for the darkness inside.
Blue in facade of red.
A cool fantasy instead of a burning reality.
Underneath lies an abyss ofintensity.
Did you truly believe her eyes to be filled with the quaintness of a fairytale sky?
That the windows of her soul reflected the towering waves of the deep ocean?
Or maybe you believed that those irises are filled with thunderclouds,
And only crackle with lightning when she's under pressure?
Such simple ideas.
Such a beautiful concept.
But she is not simple.
And her soul is not a concept.

Tarnished Memories

I sat on the railing,
the gate had rusted with the memories of a girl who believed it was an escape
when it was simply a place I visited too often in my childhood.

The top bar of the once silver railing was crumbling into brown and orange fragments of helplessness. It had been picked off by the storms we call people, and I questioned why no one else seemed to understand the kinship between metal and blood.

It was a rusted refuge,
a thing that acted like another dimension where I was free to speak the truth that I never could tell you because the gate lied on town borders.
You had no power there.

The gate would corrode with my soul as I spoke of you—
of the life you created.
The bubble that glistened in sunlight to onlookers but trapped us in our own foresight.
Yes, it blocked out all those who would destroy
my privilege,
my rights,
my rank,
and unleash the horror of humanity and war tanks.

It was a beautiful idea, in theory.
But it wasn't nearly human.

I did, however, fall in love,
like so many do when they see you.

It was as if you decorated yourself in the dreams only a human heart can fall prey to,
clothed in starlight and utopian concepts in a bed that looked like we could almost fit into.

I can never be sure if you meant for it to happen. If you did indeed turn my reflection against me or if that was my own self-discovery.

It was a day like any other where the expectations of myself were bemoaned in a classroom, but this time,
there were others.
There were whispers.
There was an audience for a secret I thought was just between you and me.

The mirage of green hills faded into sanded dunes. The lush future you grew for me had wilted in the Great Drought of Growing Up.

The shadows I mistook for friends only stood with me in sunlight. The competition I had unknowingly entered with the awkward transition of puberty become bloodthirsty—
we had lost a few souls by the time I was sixteen.
(even I lost mine in the ring of heartbreak)

The railing had seen it all, had seen your true state far before I had.
It tried to warn me,
to show me how it had been broken the same way
by a society which cared for its potential and not its meaning

I had prayed once a long time ago,
to stay a child,

to stay with you for, perhaps, forever.

But I counted forever in the lights of a burning sunset
when I should have known your forever was every breeze
that rustled the feathers of the ordinary
because you began to thrive on the matters that entail cruel entertainment.

I escaped,
albeit briefly,
by trespassing over the gate
and immediately explored the wonderfully sharp surface of a needle that could ruin your idea ofperfection.

But here is how you have been saved from me—
there are new ones you have entranced, and I'll save the needle for them

I'll bury it right underneath the pile of flaking metal from the gate so they can glance at the tarnished memories of those who came before them and understand we were all hurt.

I still go the gate to scream, sometimes.
(Just because you're living your future does not mean you've forgiven your past)

I came today to cry in secret
for all the lost things,
but it appears you've finally uncovered it.

It feels traitorous to admit,
and even more so,
it tastes bitter on my lips,
but there will always be sweetness when I say your name.

- Were you ever fond of my window light?

Midnight Revelation

I was told
I was born of
sunshine and gold

but when I came of age,
the moon finally came to me
and told me the truth

at last, the silver in my soul made sense.

- lessons in darkness

Lessons in Temptations Vol. I

if i never ran out of breath,
i would
never
stop
running
a w a y
- escape is only temporary

Lessons in Temptations, Vol. II

if it's never enough,
i've
had
e n o u g h.
- coming of age

Chasing Toxins

Leather jackets and the smell of burnt marshmallows was what I was used to.
Now there's rosé in front of me, and I've grown fond of what's sickeningly sweet to cover up the poison.
A week ago, I would stalk across the ponds littering cement, ignoring the girls who hid behind the trees.
Last night, I joined them because, in all honesty, I wanted to be free.
I think I just tasted ash, not whatever God they seemed to drink from.

Maybe it was a curse after I claimed to never disobey the rules of the true authors of my story.

Or maybe it was genetics. I'd heard the dead blood drank a liter of gin a day to wash away the sins on their bones.

Twenty-four hours and the smoke has become one with my soul.
No matter how hard I scrub, whatever darkness is there will never let go.

Who knew the dead earth had such control over young lives?
The sun's solar flares tried to whisper of Gaia's lies.
The moon, on the other hand, became brighter than the sun.
The glow on my hand was a symbol of a childhood done.

Past Lives

I know,
believe me,
I k n o w

that I was
a pirate
in another
life.

How?
You may ask.

It's simple
really.

Modern society
was, is, will be
too wicked for
the likes of
a stubborn
woman.

The ocean,
that temptress,
offers a life
of adventure
and equality
where her waves
take down
all ships

and let us
not forget
the mermaids
who lie in wait,
in pursuit of
the k i l l.

When I stowed
away
on the pirate ship,
as I know I did,

when the mermaids
sang that song
to drown us all

they found me,
a girl,
like them,
in the murky
water

eyes glazed,
sword on hip
and removed my hat
to find long locks
of blonde
cascading down my
shoulders.

The mermaid with
hair made of flames
shut her sweet lips
and unbuttoned

my shirt.

With one hand
tight and gentle
on my lower back
to hold me close—

I almost think
I can remember
the feeling of
rocking to the waves.

We do not
collectively
question
certain myths,
but we should.

We do not ask:
"how are mermaids
created?"
But we should.

I think maybe that
is why I sought after
the pirate life for me

because I knew
it was one step
c l o s e r
to someone like me

- the song from my past

The Depth of You

I can see the waves of adoration and obsession plummeting toward my spot in the sands of loneliness
Pebbles of despair blend with grains of independence, and I remind myself that to beach myself from you is my only safety
I do not look out to the horizon for I know the emotion of the ocean would entrance me like it did to all those sunken ships
The darkness of the water is so much worse than the blackness of the night, for at least the sky holds stars

In the depths of the tsunami tides lie the miserable adventure, which kills all souls, yet I cannot force myself to return to the forest
All I can do is live a pretense that the ocean is just an ocean as I sink myself lower into the sand in the name of resistance
But it is my greatest folly that I pick up the seashells of dreams whispering your name from the sea

And like that
I drowned in you

The Tides of Friendship

"I won't see them,"
ever again lingered unsaid.
As pungent as the smell of sea salt,
as unmoving as sand caught in your hair.

Is it human strength or weakness to weep like the ocean?

The rising tide of despair is one I've become accustomed to, but I did not anticipate it to swallow me whole.

I am on the ship now; I can see the bright beam spinning around dark waters. The lighthouse is calling to me, but the real light has slipped beneath the waves and into the black blanket of space.

Were these feelings made of myth and legend?

Sailors spoke tales of the mysteries held in the sea. I could not help but wonder if that mystery was you or me? For I am certain that the foreign Atlantic has altered my Pacific ways.

It is stranger to realize that it only washed away what was never there at all.

They say the deepest, darkest parts of the earth lie at the bottom of the ocean, but we both know that's false. The darkest pit science knows of is the heart.
I can feel the Marina Trench inside me, the cells of fish swimming down my bloodstream beside the tissue of plants. I'd like to believe I am more discovered than the oceanic divide, but that is just another human lie.

Can you see stars from that far beneath the surface?

From my sunken ship, I can see a faint gleam of white reflect on the metal anterior. It is the moon who makes her presence known, entrancing those I am forced to know by protocol. But she is but a speck of sand in the ocean that is the sky.

When I look harder, when I push away the top of the treasure chest, I can sometimes see those glittering wishes. I try to find my wish each night, but you escape my gaze to seek the comfort of land. The ocean is vast and chaotic, but I must call it home.

Swim away while you can, for only pirates cannot live on land.

A Picnic Down a Rabbit Hole

I truly do believe you were the reason the wind didn't blow me off the hill of desperation and false comradery.
It was so interesting to look down and realize that the masks people wore became visible only when their lives were at stake
(but we both know they were always there under a plastic smile.)

A boy would not stop watching the storybook-blessed features of your face and the pricked spindled wave of my hair. The pearl of wisdom clamped up in my throat once I realized he belonged to a different time.
They all did on that golden afternoon.

Did you notice the way the wind shifted our bodies closer? They say God created snow so that we would be bound to make our own warmth. It must be true because friends do not create sparks to keep their affection ablaze, rather they stoke the fire. But today was different.
We sat in a golden afternoon, and the Universe allowed us to peek at our future.
We could have the fake persona of a suburban life, acting as the perfect trophy wife to dust our husbands' golf clubs each morning before we meet with the societal piranhas (you acquire the skill to smell blood and weakness when you sign away your soul, you know),
We could have the foolishly safe lovers who say they'll run away but cannot bring themselves to stray from the path of what they're told,
We could have the family who was lost but at least they were lost together,
We could have us.

We could simply just have each other,
and that's enough for me.

So, yes, maybe I lied.
Maybe the wind didn't push me closer to you. Maybe that was free will even though you believe in fate.
Maybe that's why we didn't get the perfect golden afternoon and had to retreat into a bedroom where we could barely fit our personalities.
Maybe that's why I couldn't help myself from tilting my head just so. From biting my lip like that. And looking at you like we weren't cursed from the start.

Maybe we could save ourselves in the end.

Yet, that's only if you allow yourself to let the abstract concept of the relativity of time and the difference between sadness and true happiness be what it is at its core.

If you only allow yourself to be *you.*

Maybe,
just maybe,
we could get a happy ending too?

Waning Crescent of a Blood Moon

The night's aggression never has so violently slammed down a sheet of blackness on my head before last night.
God must have poked holes in the box so that I could breathe and see a glimpse of heaven, but that was not enough.
Even the devil took pity for the creatures of darkness did not lurk in the shadows, rather they sat with me.
All of us looking up,
Wondering what I had done to the universe.
I do not think that the day likes me very much, but the night and I had always made dreams together.
The night was sweet in its horrible capabilities, while the sun was cruel in its kindness to life,
But I would rather side with the dark as it was the only time I could be true to my own heart.
And to my heart I must be true, in its bloody and crimson hue,
It is a wonder that it took me so long to realize it had always belonged to you.
Maybe there were clouds that blocked my judgment, or maybe I had accidentally boarded a ship that chased the sun, and it kept me from the night everlasting.
Maybe I'm just not grown up,
But the telltale signs on my body say that's not true.

If it's any consolation,
I know the night didn't mean it,
But it doesn't change the missing moon in my heart.

The 21st Century & Me

i think
i have lived
m a n y
times before,
but
i do not believe that I
have
ever
made
it
this
far.

The Color of Wor(l)ds

When the world asks me to describe myself in hues of gold,
decorated with lines of a brilliant green,
I am not able to pick up the paintbrush and create the picture
the world so desires
The world is not a big picture but a frame for what could be,
Yet not even this larger-than-life frame could hold all of me

The waves crashing on the shore is the ocean laughing at the
world and its tedious pictures,
The picture of the perfect family,
The picture of the perfect girl,
The picture of the perfect life.
The ocean knows that all pictures can be washed away,
And so, the ocean laughs at the many people who try to
capture her in a picture

Sometimes even the sun wants me to brush up my image with
acrylic colors
He too believes in the power of pictures as no valid photo
exists without light
The sun thinks of the world as a landscape of artists who paint
a better picture,
But I cannot paint,
And I am not in this picture

It is only my beloved moon who gives me a reprieve from
daylight and the world's colorful cruelty
Instead of drawing pictures, the moon gives me words

Words of wisdom, words of advice, words of love

Words that have more power than any color could manifest by being painted on my picture

It is through these words granted by the moon that I can finally describe myself to the world
And though the lists of words could run over this world a thousand times over, there is only one word which I can say
So, when the world asks once more to explain myself to its land of conformity, I will break the paintbrushes and spill every color onto the paper before I pick up my pen and write:

Desperate

A Brief Summary of Botany

The quickest way to speak to your heart is through your own lips
Words spill out from your tongue each day, but it is your lips which wait quietly
Quivering with anticipation and every emotion, your rose-red lips garden your face to enchant someone else entirely
Sometimes your petals beckon one who likes to pick flowers, and other times, your petals call forth those who tend flowers to help them blossom like never before
The problem lies with the ordinary quality all who wander toward your garden possess.
Some may appear ethereal or mundane but each and every individual remains to be just as human as you
So how do we decipher which person to dig our roots into?
The answer is simple. Let your lips speak.
Your lips, your weapon of choice, begs to attack those who spark something beyond friendship in your veins
Thus, your lips must dance to the tune of a melody we cannot hear in its effort to find its match.

The first dance of lips I locked was when I kissed the ocean, but its waves tried to drown me
The second dance of lips I locked was when I kissed the flames of a campfire that filled my heart with smoke and left scorch marks in my lungs
The third dance of lips I locked was when I kissed a goddess who tasted of bittersweet but addicting wine that I wanted nothing but to get drunk on.
But none tasted like the light I crave

And so, I must continue to wait in the Garden of Eden,
mistaking temptations for what's right until my sunshine
breaks through storm clouds

Love & Longing

It is the feeling of nails being dragged across your skin
Leaving red lines in their wake and a ghost of pain
To which I must equate every day without you as an original sin
I sometimes believe the scars left in your wake keep me sane.

The featherlight touch of your hand in my dreams seems all too real
Each day that I do not see you only leads my mind to seeing you more
I do not know what my heart will say, but I know you will tell me to kneel
All I believe in now is to leave evidence of the stars that I tore.

I am aware that my blood is akin to a certain taste,
And I have tried desperately to stay away from ancestral chains
It is with great sorrow that I realize those efforts were to waste,
But it is with great euphoria that I can succumb to your strains.

I wonder if perhaps you cast a spell on me each night
For I cannot recall a time where I have spilled my blood for anyone but myself
You have trapped the moon in your eyes and my skin in your bite
The redundancy of love poems would be agonizing if not for your love itself.

It is with a sweet sickness that I look forward to my visions of you

Where my dreams give us a world of everlasting freedom and
eternal summer,
And it is with a clawed hand that I must rip away my dream
and heart too,
So that I can save myself from the darkest torment of an
unrequited lover.

Golden Gradient

I have fallen for demons and witches, the shadows that stand by my bed, the vampires who would not stop biting my heart,
I have fallen for the princesses and knights, the mermaids who sang to me on shore, the angels who held me in their wings
I have fallen
No, still falling
And falling further
Because I guess I've become addicted to the high of *just maybe* or the intoxicating liquor of *what if?*

By now, the doctor refuses to check my symptoms because he knows it's always the same disease. I am, instead, handed a prescription of isolation and depression, and those pills take up a lover's spot on my bed.

I see people as different colors and numbers as personalities, and I know I've accomplished the lock on my apartment
For you see, I am the only one who is so clearly Red while everyone has a gradient of colors around them. Even the demons, the angels, and the myths retained a multicolor aura of danger and passion and shyness and charisma— the blues, the pinks, the purples fading and collapsing into the other
And I stood alone in the spectrum, firmly in Red's grasp, single and excited and devastated and *hurt*
I had fallen for Blue, but sunsets always give in to darkness

Then the colors were collecting their warriors, and Red pushed me forward, and my vision was filled with Gold,
With you

You were not like the sun nor the tip of a flame. You did not burn with Hell's rage or with Heaven's light.
You were rich. Rich in imagination, in values, in strength, in beauty, in intellect, in bravery, in kindness. Rich in humanity.
I still have to stop myself from admiring you too much because you are the Crown, and I am but the blood in the water

I'm sorry that I have fallen for the Fallen
But I can't help but notice there are rubies missing from your crown?

The Tail of a High Barbary

They warn you about them when you're young—
all nails, pearl fangs,
sharp tails, sweet face,
and voices that teach you what true music is: a sweet tune hypnotizing those poor victims.
How could someone *not* go under the waves?
Because, if anything, you at least had someone to drown with.

You could say I was raised to hate them. We all were, in a way.
The Navy taught us how to tear them apart, scale by scale. Rip out the vocal cords.
What's a siren, then? Something that cannot call for help? Something that cannot cry and, thereby, use our humanity against us? Us humans.
But don't worry, we would never kill. Murder would be too kind.

I assume you were taught the same way. Draw blood if you cannot fill their lungs with water. That way, you can get the sharks to do the dirty work.

I think it's safe to say we were both indoctrinated to believe the worst of each other. Therefore, we were the worst of ourselves.

But this is international waters and my ship runs black flags instead of national stripes. And you're swimming alongside the rotted wood instead of hiding under the dark currents society has created. I can only imagine it's because you chose the pirate life for you, too.

It's true, you know. That green flash before the sun finally escapes the ocean. That one last stretch of light clinging to stay with earth. It is the light on the horizon that gives us hope, but what do we do in return?
Exist.
Exist in the dark.
That's why the light tries to stay. To see what it can never do.

To see what *we* do.

The stars know we're just chasing after the sun, even when we're in the dark, even when we claim we're after treasure. Because, in spite of the prejudice, the lies, the hatred, the despise—

We all just want the same thing. You and I know that better than anyone.

We all vehemently crave warmth, in any form, in order to make us feel *alive.* There's a difference between living and barely breathing, and that electric skin contact helps to ignite our souls. Yet, that thing the stars must feel for their galaxies on the other side of the universe must be substituted.
Enter sunshine.

I may not swim as well in darkness as you, but I can point out new suns at night?
In case you have not realized by now, we are not seeking treasure. Just something better.

A Bus Ride Away

She's not beautiful,
not out worldly so.

But inside—
inside is a survivor. Inside is a girl who has been broken and beaten.
Physically,
Mentally.
Inside there is a girl who had become so well acquainted with Death because she tried so many times to convince him to deliver her to the afterlife,
because anything
- *anything* -
was better than her current life.
But he did nothing,
So, she had to do something.
She ran

Ran away from one corrupt home to another, but this time her dad loves her.
Yet, she is still so anxious and afraid.

And I c r a v e.
I crave everything.
I crave her voice.
I crave her smile.
I crave her tenacity.
I crave her.

I don't know how it happened,

Except for the fact that I do.

I remember lying down and thinking,

“Would she love me if she knew?”

But she knows there is a demon always at my side, and she laughs along with us. The other boys and girls just hid behind white feathers.

And then there was today. And the girl who hates being touched threw me farther onto her lap, and I thought it was evidence that we could be so much more than that.

Yet. Here we are. Alone in my bed. She had left early on, but her vision is stuck in my head.

I had my arms wrapped around her. I dressed my best.
I touched her wrist here and her soul there
but nothing returned my lonely heart.

Maybe I was foolish again.

When Do We Cross the Line?

We, the people,
are fueled with gasoline
(it is truly a wonder that no one ever realized we are our own explosions.)

Change always seemed to be on the brink of jumping off the diving board but kept turning around at the sight of the pool of bodies that once looked so friendly in the shallow end but now seemed antagonistic.

We were once strangers among a campfire, but we lived like no one was watching
because for once,
they weren't.

The smell of gunpowder coated my very essence, and it is a miracle my parents never asked what crime I committed on the Fourth of July when I returned home 244 years ago.

Because, you see, I committed the most grievous of crimes:
I lost myself to freedom.

When I arrived that night, I could feel my blood hum with excitement because this was both the oldest and newest feeling one could have:
the feeling of smiling a bit more,
giving up a few more truths to a stranger,
and the desire to discover if you are who you say you are with a clouded mind.

It was unspoken that night, but the Liberty Bell rang with truth:

We are at war in every way with everyone
and even, every *thing.*

All I did was light that match and then
a roar,
an echo,
a whisper
all sounded at once.

They are coming, she warned me.

We had to race to our carriages before the soldiers tarred us as the disease we fought against was not just an infection but an addiction.
She pulled me into a pantry to tell me one last secret to which my voice was not home to the brave feeling inside,
and so, we parted for the battlefield at morning light.

I know the truth now.
We have aged in regret that melts off the tip of our tongues from words we have been too scared to say.

Forgive me,
I lost myself to a forbidden time-locked night when I was meant to be subdued by the progress of the future. Because, yes, we are here again in the present and I should be content to look upon you once more, but the past did not end with us becoming a stranger concept than friends and I cannot live in that war.

You know my colors never included white flags of forgiveness.
You always kept a spare surrender in your pocket, and I can tell you remember what killed me last time.

The Old Revolution was wicked but at least we always rose
with the Dawn.
Now we're in a Civil War, and it's only at the midnight hour
we pretend that all that's fair in love has won.

Bermuda

My darling,
I have drowned so many ships
that tried to anchor you down.
And I know,
I know,
you want to be found,
discovered,
s e e n
by someone in a way you've never been explored before.
But they would ruin your strata walls
and break the stone that I think makes you beautiful.
They would carelessly file through your past relics,
uncaring of the stories you have yet to tell.
They would claim you as theirs,
when you are so undeniably *you.*
You do not even realize how precious you are
(I am horribly thankful for that.)
If you knew that gold lined your soul, you would not be satisfied with the rusted iron in mine.
You're hiding now. Did you see the gifts I brought you?
The pretty scraps of bravery?
I don't think Amélia was trying to find you, but she got a little too close for comfort,
so I pulled her under too.
But you liked the plane?

Was it too much?
I'm sorry. I'm not good at this.
My first kiss was with a torpedo that missed his target
But you're so out of my league. Almost ten degrees above my jurisdiction, in fact.

You make the entire Pacific lust after you just by your [name] alone

But I am
feared
and cold
and alone,
and no one wants to fall in love
with what is capable of killing them

But you're here
I'm here

I know I'm doing this whole thing wrong.
I know I drowned ships you never got to board.
And I'm sorry for destroying adventures you did not get to live.

But I also know you are looking for the love of a lifetime.
Therefore,
would it be so bad to be called mine?

The Sinking

I know not of my affliction and yet God had diagnosed me at birth, hadn't he?

The Ship of Dreams they called it.
Bronzed laughter,
satin dresses,
a blue silk background for a romantic setting,
just as my parents had picked out for me.

But I did not keep to the ballroom where the taptaptaping of heels I could never wear echoed in time with the leather soles of a suitor I could never catch. Hooded eyes glanced over me like a ripple in a wave bound not for a steady shore, but for an eternity of open ocean, and that is a risk no one should take. I understand. I do. I've read the books that have shown me the arc of my character and her end, and yet, in spite of reading the same words over and over in the one small library on a ship that is powered by stardust and steam,

the story never really does justice to the truth.

The truth of the matter is that I was in the library when it sunk.

The sharp ringing of a broken violin string juxtaposed with the collapse of the steel frame quite magnificently, if I do say so myself. The first dream took, perhaps, the hardest hit as it was scraped along the seven layers of heaven (or was it hell?) that wrapped around the dream so *tightly.*
It could take five hits,

(all dreams are built with walls to protect the dreamer, you know),
most can only take two.

Hello. Nice to meet you. Yes,
you are
correct, I have indeed been:
brokenhearted and stabbed
and
neglected and burned and
misunderstood andandand—

I,
it,
we,
of course, had seven walls.

Yes, it was only one villainous wave of fire and resentment that destroyed all five walls in one go when the taptaptaping just seemed so utterly endless.

I had two more, though. I thought that would have been enough to keep afloat.

I read that this was meant to be cold, and you're right, I cannot feel my toes and my vision has mistaken the remaining lights on a sinking ship to be stars because my mind does not want to risk looking up and asking God for forgiveness after a massacre that is so clearly written in my penmanship.

The Ship of Dreams remains gorgeous even underneath the waves. I can see it still. All ripped apart and ruined and beautiful. At least I thought it was.

I'm aware that the water morphs our perception, but I could use the thin layer of ice that was spreading between my fingers to see how powerful every vision I had
was,
is,
could be,
even under my curse of darkness.
If I could just reach—

"***HELP!***"

That's not what angels sound like.
Sirens maybe?
No.

In fact, that sounds a little like *me.*

Dreams always take us under.
I just never expected to drown
for two hours and forty minutes.

P.S. tell the Carpathia I'm sorry.

P.P.S. No, I did not think of the other passengers when I set sail.

The One That Got Away

Everyone reminisces over the One That Got Away
But what of the One?
She escaped your claws of possession only to escape another.
Mankind paints her in the light of beauty and mayhem,
forgetting she is just a girl who wanted to be loved.
Not owned.
So yes, she is the One That Got Away—
And for good reason too. How could you expect a modern woman to live in the medieval ages? Better yet, we must ask how medieval women did not murder every man who ever demeaned and hurt them.
Regardless, look at you on your white horse in your jeweled attire. The crown on your head glimmers in the reflection of the sunset.
The peasants marvel at you, and you know you love it.
Yet, your eyes linger on the One. The girl running away from you as fast she can, toward the shadowlands.
A lesser evil.
A new girl in the crowd has already caught your eye. This will be your Queen.
And people will tell tales of you and your wife, but the fairytale of the One will haunt children's bedsides forevermore.

- which one of us is *really* cursed?

The World We Live In (& With)

If the body
is a temple
then why do
s o m a n y
defy the gods?

- "1 in 5 Women Are Sexually Assaulted"
a statistic from the survivors who speak up.

Woes of Public Education

Those who have broken hearts do not wish to inflict the same pain onto others.
Most times.

I have the peculiar situation of wanting to burn out the love someone has for me.
Treating it like the infection that it is,
and rebirth from the ashes truly is the only cure.

The problem is
you can’t help people who don't want your help.

At a young age,
children are taught of hatred
because the world is not made of gumdrop buttons or sugar plum fairies,
it is made of something darker.
And darkness, like love, is a cold that spreads quickly.

Children are told,
“You cannot make people love you.”
A sentiment you do not really learn the meaning of until the “I love you” isn’t returned.
It is a gut-wrenching feeling of utter despair,
but at least children are warned.

They do not teach children
how to say “I do not love you”
because these children are not supposed to break hearts
but to fall in love too—
just as every fairytale propaganda has produced.

I would like to help.
Yet, it will be easier for everyone if I break your heart
before you know that it is broken.

That way
when you finally know the truth,
it won't hurt much
because you'll know
I never deserved you.

- I promise to make it quick

Define Human for Me

There is a desire in me that compels my hands to rip off my own clothes so that I may be bare of protection and, instead, inflict upon my irises the figure I once so detested
To look once more in a silver dimension to see a marble Aphrodite whose arms have been broken off from her own unkind self-loathing.
You see, love they taught. But standard education remains to be memorization.
To learn to appreciate the curve of a woman or to caress a bump of the stomach instead of penalizing the health of anyone but yourself is the subject I have found myself studying in the Library of Alexandria.
But the Library was burned long ago, and all we have now are ashes and embers that start a new fire of prejudice.
Why do you think society demeans such a beautiful entity that is a woman's body?

Even today, I find myself caged by my own childhood indoctrination that veils my truth to the real world.
And when I enter a closet and find the courage to strip myself and bear witness to the sin that is my supposed flesh and bone,
When I find that Artemis had the right idea to run away from mankind,
Why must it always, *always* be Zeus who forcefully separates me from the darkness that he condemned me to in the first place? Why is it his hands that have the right to run down my spine and clutch at my waist?
Athena, my goddess, can you do the curse again? Medusa is left alone, but I do believe she would like a friend,
Or a lover.
I can be both, I promise.

Yet, you ignore my devotion because of my kinship to the goddess of love. She birthed me, Athena. I cannot help the pearl dust smears on my skin nor the everlasting sea salt in my hair.

It is fine.

Eventually, Hades came to me in the darkness when I escaped from Zeus.
He taught me how to make hellfire in my veins and now, the Sky King is afraid, too.
Persephone grew me a crown of thorns and daffodils so that all may know my reign over my vessel.
So now I stand in a dimension plated gold and find that human softness is what gods were so scared of—
for the beauty of the body is our only weapon against the ethereal.

The Apocalypse We Know Now

I was made for the end of the world.

Here we are:
the Dying,
the Sick,
the Helpless,
Us

And the world is shooting bullets of pandemonium, which ricochet off already bloody and bruised flesh.
The silver lockdown is now freedom.
The open fields are now green dungeons.
Because the earth was always a tool we use on the government's workbench, never thinking we could accidentally hurt ourselves in the process of the project we called "progress."
How many days have we been rotating around the media and mistaking it for the sun?
How many days have we plucked up our supposed courage when we've only torn out grass from our future graves?
How many times have we drowned creatures in their own watery habitat because we were running out of gas on our way home from work?

The time has come.

The ice has melted.
The atmosphere has thinned.

The world is dead.

And we are still picking at her corpse for scraps.

But there still lie young in her coffin, for she knew they did not cause her suffering. For twenty years, I have rested on her bones without knowing my Mother was already gone.

There are screams in the graveyard. The skeletal war rages on even though there is no glory in hell.

It seems there is nothing like Death that makes us feel so *alive.*

And I believe my Mother knew that. Maybe that's why she surrendered. Maybe that's why she said goodbye.

However,
there is a daffodil growing on my ankle, its vine sprouting around my leg. I cannot help but think that the end has come,
Just not for you and me
Or our friends, the stars in the sky.

The Hunt Down

I imagine
It was Psapfo
Who taught me how to approach
The girl in sheep's clothing

The violet
Stood proud among greener grass,
But it didn't explain our situation

It was just a hint,
Just a warning,
Like Afroditi herself wanted me
To banish my feelings for the moon in my sky

Stars can take the moon's place
For a moment,
I can beselfish

It was predatory,
And I did not know I had it within me,
An animal of finer taste

The shepherd was younger,
And perhaps,
More beautiful
Than the moon that ignored my night

I was never fond of tulips,
But they covered the girl's lips,
And I guess I can search
For sweet nectar in a kiss

There was sweat born out of malice,
Of jealousy,
And desire
That stained a sacred face
On Afroditi's wooden altar

Her job was to guard sheep
From a wolf
I think she must have forgotten
To guard her love from me

Tattoos I Won't Regret

i like the feeling of my
s k i n

better when the ink has bled
i n.

- wounds from a writer's pen

Medusa's Side

In front of the judges, those friends of Death,
I knew I could not lie
Nor did I really want to

King Hades was there, his hand on my shoulder
As if to say, "It's better this way."
I contemplated my answer as the spark heated Hell.
Persephone, gorgeous in every way, sat there
Seemingly bored, but her eyes held that glint—
The glint of mischief in her emerald irises
Staring down the God who was their king,
Daring him to say he was *her* king

My shoulder burned briefly
Licked by the flames of Tartarus
Punishment for hesitation, but the king
Hades did not seem to be listening
The drone of rights and wrongs by Minos, Rhadamanthys, and Aeacus
Continued like a plea for help
Yet, the God of Death was too lost in the gaze of Life,
Too entranced by Light's defiance against its surrender to Darkness

The tales make out the Underworld to be fueled by a bonfire of horror,
But they forget the power of the flames of love that heat up this world with something *more.*
I was not one of the judges that stood before the Doors of Death, but I could judge the pair
His gaze was soft, tender as the first kiss against her look of passion.

It was the truest kind of love, the one people are scared of,
Which is why it makes sense that they were hidden away from the rest of the universe
Not even the other gods could manifest such a state of adoration,
Thus, they condemn it to the deepest pits of Hell.

Hades understood my plight that began with that same look,
The feeling of helplessness to a greater force than anything I could fight,
Persephone, I suspect, could relate as well and so,
With the purest of intentions in the darkest of times,
The goddess inclined her head and followed *him* with hooded eyes,
The demigod I had refused to eviscerate walked forward.

He looked more Godly than any of the Olympians reigning the mountain,
Even with the shy glance to his surroundings,
The demigod retained an aura of golden strength as warm as his smile,
It was one of the things I hated most about the Adonis,
But it was not the reason I refused to tear the man apart.
Hades stood before me as Persephone pushed the demigod closer,
And despite the glory and bravery embedded in his veins,
Even *he* could not help but hesitate on his journey to my side;
I had chosen Death, but Death had not chosen me.

I was cursed to love him by the devious Aphrodite herself,
Except the demigod was not cursed to love the monster with vipers on her skin.
The cold blessing by my friend Athena had been appreciated once,

But now it was my own heart that I had accidentally turned to stone.

Perseus was a mere visitor in the shadowlands,
Enticed by the treasure Hades had spoken of,
Confused when he found himself facing the monster he killed.

"The treasure?" the demigod asked
Hades tilted his head and said, "In front of you."
"You are mistaken, my Lord. That is just the creature I killed."
Hades wandered leisurely my way with a smirk on his lips,
With a wave of his hand, the enchantment lifted to reveal the face of a girl.

The demigod stepped back in alarm, but Hades simply laughed,
The hero could face beasts but not those who were capable of smiling back,
It was with bittersweet irony that the demigod had more trouble comprehending my human form.

"Do you not recognize the woman sweet Delphi predicted you'd love?"
The silence from the hero was almost unbecoming as he processed the information.
I watched helplessly, feeling insecure without the constant hissing on my shoulder,
Persephone raked her sharp nails on my lower back, making me squirm further.
King Hades grew tired with the young man's emotional state and shoved him,
"Where's your courage, Perseus? What is so frightening about love?"

But the King of the Underworld did not know this kind of Hell.

Starstruck

I believe I understand how that lone planet on the edge of our solar system must feel,
forever watching as We spin round and round, life gravitating in ways that defy the laws of science as we know it.
That lone planet, with only the ice as its friend to shield it from the horror we have created,
sits,
watching,
mesmerized by that which is so simple to Us.

Can you even imagine?
Sitting there for billions upon billions of years with nothing but the flirty winks of passing meteors to grace it with some kind of light in its life?
And then there is Us.
There is Earth.
Basking in the sun's glory, swinging around the star just enough for a playful kiss of summer before teasing into the darkness for winter.

Do you not think the other planets noticed?
Do you not believe in the jealousy they hold for the planet who seduced the sun?
No other planet was gifted with life. With the never-ending stories and adventures and romance and woe.
With Us.
But like Earth, you do not see Us.
Like Pluto, I am forced to watch you ignore that which is right in front of you.

Lovestruck Spring Thunderstorms

Trying to understand love, I've concluded, is like trying to see out into darkness. You think you know what's out there. You think you can even see the outlines of the tree in the backyard or the rolling hill you know resides in the distance. You know it's there, so you convince yourself that you see it, but you don't actually. It's called "the dark" for a reason. The black sky isn't supposed to be a familiar blue. Love is certainly not a familiar emotion despite what humanity may believe. You may think you know your heart's desire. You may think you see the outline of the guy or girl of your dreams, but you'll soon wake to find it was plebeian heartbreak. Love isn't something you can control. Nor does it like to be seen. Love likes the dark. Love *is* the dark.

A Summer Yet to Live

When I used to think of feelings or of my heart,
I saw rage and darkness, and I believed it to be the stellar compilation of a little thing called "love."
I romanticized my demons and cast out my own god because the sins that wrecked my flesh made me hurt
Just
A
Little
Less.

And my past lovers, you should know, were driven by the same factor.
I was a thing,
and a *thing* is all they needed to satisfy their lust

I did not—
more so,
could not—
believe in that little thing called love.

I could never fathom mathematics and to lure one body into one bed to combine two souls to create and multiply miracles in a division of two hours of free time we had before someone returned back to a 15-year-old dorm room
That is a Lorentz equation, and I only wanted art.

I just—
I want—
I need.

SOMETIMES, I HAVE A HEART

When I think of you, I could never so clearly before picture summer.

Not of an ocean breeze on a crowded beach,
nor the suffocating splashes from children in an overly chlorinated pool,
Not of melting ice cream that makes your hands stick,
or of a humidity that makes you sweat from one step outside, heavy breathing already cued.

I think of rolling golden hills. Dead grass that makes the scenery somehow even more beautiful.
I think of farmers' markets and taking a bite of fresh fruit, the juice slipping onto my lips.
I think of flowers that I have never liked but still dream of holding them close because they were a misunderstanding like me.
I think of crickets singing in the night, shouting from the top of their lungs about the one they love, because they set an example we all should follow.
I think of you, throwing me onto a bed with the window open and sunlight streaming in. I think of you, and it's fresh and new but it's also an archaic bond that's sweet and bitter *and, and, and—*

I don't know what it is.
I haven't felt like this before.

It's not pretty,
I would wager it's rather ugly,

But it's also intoxicating, and I can't stop my mind from slipping away, getting drunk off the thought of you.

I don't know what it is.

I know what it is.

You care about me
And that's the most romantic thing anyone has ever done.

A Universal Secret

people say i love you to the moon and back,
but i love you much, much more than that
you are my sun, my gravity, my light anew,
i, the moon, incapable of shining without you

Tin (Wo)Man

My lips keep twitching,
they know there was a job they were born to do,
I checked out too early when we had a lifetime,
but how can I work myself back to you?

My heart's overworked
because my blood is the only thing keeping me warm,
and my love is underpaid
because I had to cut the costs myself.

The assembly line might have worked on others,
but it doesn't seem to be building me back up again.
This heart feels just like the last one:
it fucking *hurts*

How can I already be bleeding oil? What happened to the ink?

I thought I could spit out stories. Instead, I'm coughing up ash, and
the smokestacks almost seem like they're signaling you,
trying to save me from me.
But I know you don't want me to pollute your skies, and I'm so sorry I can't go clean.

I didn't realize I was running on black energy.

I didn't realize there were more important things (than what I believed society dictated of me).

I didn't realize your yellow petals were becoming burnt. That *I* was burning them long before the earth got hotter.

Regardless, you still held onto me.
Me, this *thing* that could destroy you.
That wanted to, at one point.
The gears were rusted, and I didn't bother to fix my problems
because I thought I'd be converted soon enough.

I was wrong.

A Philosophy

I find that
L o v e
has many faces.

Love is the warrior
hesitating to strike
against the knight.

Love is the friend
that leaned in
a little too close.

Love is the demon
dancing in your
shadow all night.

Love is the thief
stealing allthings
precious to you.

Love is the student
learning how to
make their way.

Love is the God
who has no clue
what they're supposed to do.

Love is that *thing*
you feel
when the fire is not stoked,
but we're being warmed by something all the same.

No Other Word

I mistook the sunflower for you again.

how could I not?

it loved sunshine just as much as you,
stood out among the crowd like you,
lived,
breathed,
dreamed summertime like you.

It had to be you.

so, I ran because I screwed up our past lives,
(and it shouldn't take an infinity of lifetimes to make me be a better person)
I tore through Sappho's beloved violets,
Virginia's darling roses,
(do you remember being Vita?)
and Emily's pretty tulips
(I jumped around Jane's daffodils, of course, just in case we left a bit of our souls in her garden across the pond)

none of the women seemed to care, though. I was an antagonist trying to trade roles and how utterly fascinating that must have been to see a villain love.
they just watched as sharp green blades cut into my paper ankles,
nature against human nature,
trying to stop me from being reckless

but I think you loved it most when I threw my fears of "what next?" into the wind. Eventually the breeze came back, but you'd shut the window of a third-floor dorm and watching the moon was all that mattered.

It was so—
what's the word?
cute seems too juvenile
precious seems too poetic for a self-aware poem.
maybe I better stick with the word that I always associated with you:
Lovely.
Yes, you were lovely,
and in consequence, it was lovely to see you
it was lovely to see your eyes be so taken with the moon
when in fact, you were sunshine incarnate

Apollo lost you when you were born,
don't worry, Artemis made sure you blossomed in the light of day
(but the moon kissed you goodnight).

I reached the sunflower,
it wasn't you.
Again.

Artemis loves you
(rightfully, obviously, how couldn't she?)
but I think Aphrodite hates me

- maybe we were meant for myths

Star-Crossed Lovers

I can't stop myself from shaking.
And sweating.
And I don't think my heart has ever beat so fast before.

I haven't heard your voice since the sun collapsed in on itself.
I had to use a star from a distant galaxy for non-existent warmth.
I made myself believe that space was just a blanket of nothing.
That it didn't possess anything worth having.

But that's not true.

Space has these lost souls called stars.
Space has these planets we call home.
Space has me and you.

I should have recognized that I packed meteors in a backpack, not shooting stars.

I guess it didn't matter in the end, though.

You still took a ring from Saturn and placed it on your finger. I had a wine bottle full of dark matter that you gave meaning to. We can drink from it, once more? We haven't opened it for a millennium but everything you touched never lost its sweetness.

I wonder if the stardust on your lips tastes like the wish I wanted. Regardless, I think reality might be kinder than the fantasy of us.

The Beginning of the End

The cradle of heaven broke itself upon the Garden of Eden.
You may have believed that it was love that caused the beginning of life, but you forget that lust is a sin.

The blood of the covenant now rests itself upon an ashen pentagram in the stars while the waters of the wombs have drowned out the potential for anything "good."
Sometimes, I find the warmth of the flames of Hell to be just the right temperature. It's warm enough to melt the ice in my heart but not enough to deplete my very soul. While Heaven retains light strong enough to blind the innocent and resurrect them as demons in cloaks of white.

Eve understood that quite quickly when she was forced to be with a man who could not tell a sunrise from a sunset on their day of existence. Eve, bare of cloth and of humility in the Lord's plan, defied her own destiny as a result of lust. Of love.

Seduction is an art few can master but, of course, the Fallen can only bring others into the shadows with them. And so, Lucifer drew Eve the picture of happiness with the bones of God's dead dream. And so, she loved it. And so, she lusted it. And so, she sinned.

And so have I.

A Frightening Innocence

There is something,
something about me
that scares Death to his
spirit core. I assume it is
the pixie dust that I have poured
out of my heart and onto the floor.
I am a child who runs with nymphs
and cries with the clouds.
I sing along with the mermaids
who lie at the bottom of the pool.
I do not kiss frogs though,
I know I am too young for such
a commitment. The crown would be
too heavy on my little head
(but that never stopped anyone
else).

I believe—
as I always do—
I do believe in fairies, I do, I do.
I believe that such an innocence
emitting out of tiny crystals
is an alarming reality
Death did not want a chance
encounter with. And so, I *believe*
in absolutely everything.
But above all,
the good in the world.

I believe I am a Pirate
and no tyrant government
institution could enforce its

sexist damsel in distress policy
on my tiny limbs.

I believe I am an Explorer
and ancient relics left secrets
just to whisper to me. No snakes
could deter me from the museum
of my own dreams.

I believe I am a Historian
diving down into the depths of
another world entirely. Just to see
the truth, the evidence, the fact
that nothing is unsinkable.

I believe I am alone
in the regard that my imagination
is something that helps
me to see both angels
and demons.

I believe I am a human,
but then fiction grips me in
a plush, red seat.
There is a woman
who seems so kind,
so beautiful,
so
Broken.

I want to fix her
even though she wants
to break me into pieces
so I could never

become anything
but her *doll.*

I almost want to do it,
you know,
I want to rip out
those orbs that connect me
to a life I do not really like
and let her do with me as she will.
It makes more sense to be here
then to be over there.

I can tell I have
absentmindedly so
ripped apart her web of a home.
The one she wove for me with such
care. They all say she just wants
to catch me, but I cannot
help but feel she wants
someone to love.

For webs can only hold so many
dewdrops until they break
but twice the force means
the victims will never escape.

Coke has been spilled on
my seat, but I let my arm stick
to it just so that I cannot move—
(exactly like she wants.)
I am hypnotized for the first
but certainly not the last time.
Paralyzed by seeing myself
in a large reflection,
wondering who could have

captured me on screen without
my knowledge.

February 7, 2009—
a Saturday that was hot
In spite of the chill of my story.
A day that I realize
everything I believe in—
the magic, the love, the *good*
is nothing but artificial
chemicals I left untouched
in my palm. The candy may
have tasted sweet, but it is
still toxic to my essence.
I believe I am brave,
and I suppose I am because
I never saw the end of the story.
But I knew the beginning.
I knew the parents that were never home,
the bully who would never leave me alone,
and the other world that was just so utterly
Tempting.

I believe that the power
of good will always defeat evil.
At least I did,
but now I know
Good isn't worth believing in
when it's so easy for the bad guys
to win.
- a kid who is still scared of the dark

How the Mighty Fall

You showed me the euphoria of running away,
The freedom associated with defying society was like drinking stars from the never-ending bottle of space
I could not be bound to reality when fantasy was so beautiful
You showed me the *I love you*'s, which tucked me in each night also chained me to the monster under my bed
I did not see you slowly sink your teeth into my bounds, breaking my tethers before I could hesitate
I did not see you push the bottle of stars and galaxies and black holes deeper into my mouth until I was choking,
No one is meant to overdose on that which is not real and yet you were a drug that I had not realized I was addicted to.
You showed me the liberation of running away but left out the effects
The heart I had begun to crack
My vision went from rose to violet
The cloud above my head grew heavy with lightning strikes

It was not until we reached the destination of nowhere that I saw nail marks you scratched onto my skin,
I saw the invisible bite that marred the base of my neck
I saw the bloodstains that ravished my clothes
I saw the spiked tail that bound my wrists to you

I sat there, dumbfounded with the knowledge that the pretty angel who had set me free from my Hell,
The angel who gifted me with enchanting prose and a starlit smile, who wrapped feathered wings around my shoulder to shield me from myself,
Was Fallen.
Corrupted.

On the pathway to a demoness, tricking me into seeing light
when there were only ever shadows.
You were the monster all along, trying to drag me down to
your new home with you. The worst part is
I loved the thrill of the fall.

The Truth of Dreams

my head is full of fantasies
and
nightmares,
but i cannot tell which one is which.
- they are both called dreams in the end

The Dying Days

How alone do you have to be to crave poison?
I thought I simply wanted to kill myself, but self-murder is not
simple.

I thought I knew Death, but I think he only knows me,
it is a one-sided love story that I don't have the energy to
complete.

I was born a paradox and will die an enigma—
a child of light with darkness in her heart,
a woman scared of the dark but more so
of the bright colors popping out of the art
in the museum of Found Souls she ought to know.

I reckon it's because neither Satan nor God wanted to risk the
safety of their kingdoms for the girl who was capable of—
smiling while the man slit her wrists and carved out her lungs
(because who needs to breathe air when you can breathe
blood?)
kissing the girl who pushed her off the edge of the bruised
cliffs of self-confidence and into the family shark nest,
time,   and time,   again
(because trust is a two-way street, and the cobblestone lanes
are meant to be claustrophobic)
or hugging the monster that ripped apart her quaint bed of
hopes and cinched her land of dreams
(because, to be frank, nightmares always win).

I have a plan—
a plan to die
a plan to live

but those plans often get confused with one another, and I'm
afraid they've gone and switched their timing.

If I had to diagnose myself, I would say it's all the symptoms of
a broken heart.
The trouble is, this heart has been broken since the very start
of my low-level existence on a plane that hates my very being.

I do not know where the Grim Reaper will take me,
but I don't expect that we will go very far—
I know whatever force that loathes me
will want to play with me in the stars.

Lessons in Temptations, Vol. VI

Even God loved the Devil once

- we all fall for our demons

The Road to Insanity

Chaos likes to drive a stake into your heart as gently as a lover's caress
Chaos likes to rip scars into your flesh so that its victims may feel littered in kisses
Sanity is there, of course, watching from inside your mind, clawing at the wall that grows thick at the sight of chaos
Sanity screams so loud that your mind can no longer recognize any other sound, thus you lose hearing and rely on sight
The sight of such a beautiful and intoxicating darkness that it lights up your life
It is inevitable that you will give into chaos. You are, after all, only human.
But chaos does not last forever, and time is the true heartbreaker.
The clock will tick while you are removed from chaos. The wounds dressed as hickeys marking your skin will fade.
Even your reflection will unfortunately look normal.
You can try to pretend you did not succumb to chaos, but the return of sanity's voice will never
Ever
Let you forget the time you lost yourself,
And not even chaos could inflict that much pain.

Lessons in Temptations, Vol. III

fight

F I R E

with

H E L L F I R E

- burning bridges isn't the only option

Sinner

I feel like I can only exude sin
The darkness, the wrath, the
corruption—
is the only thing that's within.
I do not credit myself a Satanist, but I do believe God has lost all faith in me.
I know the angels tried to hold me down with ropes bathed in holy oil, but that only made me bleed from the inside out.
They kissed me, but their lips were too dry, and their kisses too stiff
when I tried to add tongue, they could not tolerate the taste of me.
But when I kissed my demons, they knew just how to love,
burned and pulled down and *wanted,*
and hell became a h(e)aven.

The flames of hell are leaking out of my soul, but I do not know how it got in. I suspect it happened when my knees were forced onto the steps of a marble altar for a confession I didn't admit to.

There's a crown of thorns I'm meant to wear, but the only throne that counts anymore is the body.
They sacrificed my sanity for me during the coronation, and you can see it in the remains of the peace they brokered off from my flesh so that veins of chaos were all that was left.

The Devil would never have forgotten my rejection, but the fangs in my neck aren't as sharp as I remember them in my nightmares.
A bite, just a small one, to test my pain tolerance.
I can only hope She does not find it in the ashes of a burned-up love letter.

I think God is disappointed in me, but at this point, it's all for naught.
Grace and holiness and forgiveness and redemption—
all just words a priest said to get a kid under the palm of his hand
that slid down farther.
I did not ask for forgiveness;
I did not ask for this.

At least the Devil asked for my consent.

The 22 Reasoned Theses

I have taped a confession letter to your door, and I regret it.
Burn it.
Rip it to shreds.
Run it over and make sure you hit me in the process.

I was immature. I thought I should be honest, but adulthood is about lying, and if I was mature, I would have known.

I was foolish, chasing after the idea of romance when Cupid has been evading me all his life, so why would he stop his ways now?

I even tried to turn my attention onto someone else, but it wasn't like with you, it wasn't the easy flow of conversation, and I now recognize that's what you call friendship, and I've ruined it.

But I think you wanted me to ruin it anyway. Just not for a romantic purpose.

You wanted an excuse to *run.*

This kingdom of fire is too much for your forest blood roots. I am but a Knight of Flames, and you're afraid that a simmer is all it takes to burn you to the ground. Couldn't you trust me?

The forest may not always be there, and you're jealous of the Ocean, so fire is all that's left, sweetheart. You have a choice to side with it or against it, but you've chosen to treat the kingdom's act of kindness as an act of war all because we do not understand your seasons.

So, go ahead and do it. Leave now. Leave forever.

You're welcome for the push.

Lessons in Temptations, Vol. V

You are
the kind
of person
who inspires
P o e t r y

- but that's not always a good thing

Lesson One: Heartache

The worst way to break someone's heart is to make them believe you loved them, too

- "I love you" was the cruelest thing you could have ever said

Watercolor Tears

writing on napkins
and wiping away
a day of makeup
is the only form of art
i can illustrate

- an artist who cannot paint except for the canvas of a sad face

The Lost Summer

There is a hill that the sun likes to rest on
every sunset.
Just a pause,
Just a moment,
Where he can shine brightly one last time
before the moon takes the nightshift.

Never have I seen someone run up that hill
instead of marvel at the pink romance in the sky.
But you did.

You ran up instead of down,
head down instead of up,
red cheeks instead of tears
bit lip to block out fears—
the fear of kissing a girl
(because Texas taught you love was a sin).

Now, I cannot stand the sunset.
It is a reminder that every dusk was meant to be ours
alas, only the moon can kiss the sun.

Now, *I* have the nightshift,
and skeletons from my closet have become my only company.

The cemetery of my broken hearts needs a new caretaker.
I thought it could be you,
but I guess I must throw another funeral for another lost love.

The ghosts of my memories still haunt the grounds.
I tried to sprinkle holy water, but God said this was a fitting
punishment.

Roses have wilted on the graves of those I have given up on.
If you cared to know, I put fresh lilies on your coffin.

I was meant to bury my heart six feet deep,
and the grave has been dug, you made sure of it,
but the coffin is unlocked, and I can hear my heart still beat
for you.
If you want to bury my love alive, I guess I should bury myself
too.

Lessons in Temptations, Vol. IV

it wasn't until you placed a knife in my heart,
twisted it for good measure,
that i realized
you
loved
me
too.

- but we were each other's poison.

Unrequited

i sort of thought you would be with me at the end of the world
instead, souls from the river styx are dying again just to drag
me in,
and you're in another myth entirely

- we could have made the underworld a home

Margin Notes

I believe that if we knew what occurred after life,
everyone would commit suicide.

The golden landscapes where you can frolic among the angels and the stars,
perhaps stop for a pot of tea and a chat with God—
why wouldn't you take a knife?
why would you willingly endure more pain,
and suffering
and complete and utter heartbreak,
if you were aware that after making that decisive action
you would be *happy*.

Imagine—
the blood is a little frightening at first. The red liquid is seeping out of your wrists, and you don't feel altogether whole.
(but then again, did you ever in life anyway?)
Your vision begins to tunnel but the fear drives off into the distance.
Then you see someone.
"Oh, good day, Mr. Reaper. How do you do?"
And with a skeletal kiss to your knuckles, he leads you on through to that thing, that place, that frozen point in time that happens after life.

Gates that shine with something akin to sunlight reveal themselves among cotton-dusted clouds.
And there, waiting for you, are all the ancestors you've never met but who always watched you.
They stand smiling,
awaiting you with open arms
with the love you never received in life.

There are familiar faces, too. The old teacher you had in kindergarten waves. The grandfather you never got to meet kisses your cheek and ruffles your hair.
It is *warm.*
Warmer than the 112-degree summer days that you holed yourself up by an air conditioner when your friends all went to the pool without you.
Warmer than the flames that burnt your marshmallow completely in your quest to make a s'more as the ghost stories became more intense, but you realized you had ghosts of your own to worry about.
Warmer than the first flush of butterflies you got when your crush acknowledged your presence before he immediately turned the other way to laugh at the joke his jockeys just made about you.

It's warm in the way that you would imagine a tangible "good" would feel
And if this truly is the afterlife, why stop me from wanting warmth?

NOTE:
***Maybe it's because the cold teaches you how to live**

Bloom in Blood

"I love you" slipped out of your mouth like it was a wisp of a cloud spitting out of what you call a sunshine smile, but the sharp teeth glimmer with the threat of midnight moonlight. Even the taloned branches that cling to the Tree of Life have broken off by the sound of your voice alone.

How have you seeped your hands into the archaic roots of a tree that should never know you exist? It's rotting from the inside out despite the tender way you run your hands through its groves, and I can't help but understand how nature feels helpless to you.

Take it back.

Take back the way you kiss the blossoms that only come out when they believe it's safe for them to revel in their dark hues.
Take back the way you lie down on watered-down pebbles in the stream to make them sharper with your uncut affection.
Take back the way you say "I love you" as if it was honey that I'm not allowed to kiss off your lips.

"I love you" is not what makes you dangerous,
it's the predator waiting.

It's the warped value system in your head that puts a kiss between two humans as a bond meant for two souls created by the same star but that the holding, the wanting, the rocking, the *desire* involved in the planting of oneself into another's body is commonplace.
I am not common. Love is not either.

You forget that, in spite of the garden you trick into growing
for you—
The roses, the daffodils, the thyme, the basil, the bluebells, the
strawberries, the—
What was her name again? I've forgotten because it's been so
long since you planted someone new over her;
I am human too.

And I do not grow for you. I am perfectly happy in my own
blood.

Heartbreak is Ancient History

A bolt is just a piece used to secure machine work,
to make sure every gear is set in place and runs smoothly,
just as the blueprint you wrote up intended.

I was a fool who inhaled too many toxins from the fury and exploitation of the Industrial Revolution that was occurring inside your head.

How had I not realized that you were doing the mummification process?
Yet, we were not in Ancient Egypt, and you were not ruling a country, but you were ruling me.
I thought I was the brave lover, and I thought you were removing my armor so that you could push me down on satin silk with ease, but you treated the metal as something that was far more precious than Marc Anthony and me.
Caesar and I, perhaps, have more in common than I originally thought. We both were stabbed by our court, and it is only beyond the grave that I retain the memory of laughter, and I believe I was, in fact, the jester. Your jester. The jester that was once a knight before you stripped off the metal and transformed human sentiment into a laughing matter.
Was my armor sufficient for you, my demoness?

I saw you slip past the curtain in the corridor beyond the throne room to satisfy your hunger in the arms of an enemy of yours, and I cannot help but wonder if that situation derived purely out of curiosity or in spite?
Were you curious of my reaction? Or did you just want to spite the supposed "goodness" a knight like me is meant to represent?

I would rather slit my own throat than confirm to you that you successfully injected poison in my veins.

You've lost your crown now, but I see you occasionally when we are forced into the Neutral Zone in the war of life.

The armor is gone, of course, you melted and melded it to replace the spot where your heart once laid so no one could accuse you of not having one (a metal one still ordered oxygen to be placed in blood but saved you of all the dreaded emotions).

I was cast out of knighthood, but the sword is inked onto my wrist so that I may reach for a knife up my sleeve at a moment's notice. A lesson that you taught me and I will not thank you for.

I have hated, and I do hate, and I will hate you for the rest of my being. The bolt you gave me was a clear symbol of your opinion of me.

But I will forever hope that it at least came out of the machine you call a heart so that I can know you loved me,
at least at one point in time.

Diary Documentaries

I am cursed to love and be unloved in return
- The repeated diary entries that God will never learn
April 2016 May 2019 March 2020

The Witch in the Night

You're the reason that the next time someone tells me they love me, I won't be able to believe them. So, thank you for that lesson.

You've ripped up the word, letter by letter, picking up the pieces around you so that you could build the dream in your fantasy, but you forget that it was my nightmare.

If I were to ask you why you claim to love me, I know you'd say it was because of the pretty words I'd write and the lovely things I'd say.
But you forget I am a writer, and this is a work of fiction.
You were the poem I had been writing and writing and writing until I realized some words do not belong in the vocabulary of our story:
Love
Lust
London

Regardless,
actions have always spoken louder than words.

*

You see,
it was just a normal day

And then I was confronted with a magic I mistook for something pure, but it was actually just a curse from a red book
I woke up on my own because the princess who was supposed to kiss me awake was also the one who put me asleep.

Now I sit on a throne of ripped up paper, and my kingdom of stories reads ours over and over to warn their children of "true" love

A damsel in distress?
Their ruler, a "sweet rose?"
She was a daffodil in a brutal British winter.
Those that loved the Garden of Eden remembered.

I guess that is why the dragon won.

It may be a flowery detail of the story, but I believe the end with angels' tears did not compare to the laughter of demons. (The part where Hell kept the Queen company was my favorite. She grew so much as a character.)

Because, as you may remember,
the words and lines,
the lives and lies,
the kingdom and war,
the curse and sword,
created a cautionary tale of a witch in your wake.

You are old enough to know this now—
some fairytales don't get happy endings.
At least,
not with me
and my kingdom of stories.

Myths of Manifesting

I walked back into Hell with the stench of spite healthily stronger.
Hades stepped down from a throne made of bones and shadows pulled out from Tartarus and handed me the deed to your grave plot.
I ripped up the papyrus scroll because a soul lost for eternity was the kindest mercy I could do for a person who lied about love.

Persephone held Jesus' crown of thorns in her hands, letting it scar away at golden flesh as it did when it was shrouded in roman mythology.
When I did not move, the goddess placed it on my head and let her nails scrape at the bottom of my neck in warning because religion does not peacefully coexist.

The dark gleam in his eye told me that the King of the Dead and the Undead was filled with pride for the soldier that returned victorious from the most wicked of battlefronts in that of the cruel affairs of the heart.
But the crease in her brow told me that the Queen of Life was consumed with an overpowering surge of disappointment that all but rolled out of her strained smile upon my return. The words didn't exit her tongue, but the clenching of her teeth was so saturated in shadows that they dripped the words "you

did

not

live."

And maybe I hadn't.
At this point, who has?

Her husband and I knew the crucifixion did not matter anymore. Gods can only do so much but changing the past isn't one of them.
So, to the future, to the Underworld, to the mission of destruction and chaos and placing the fear of Hellfire into the souls that were fortunate enough to cross my path—
This prayer, darling, is for you.

(Isn't it funny how you feast on the flesh of Christ and sip on his blood in the pew of an institution you never believed in, yet you refuse to kiss the lips of a lover because *that* is too intimate?

Don't worry, Hell hath made your loathing love my punishment.)

Down to a Science

Why do the words "I love you" from your lips hurt more than the knife you stabbed in my gut
(was it to keep me from recognizing my senses)?
Love is supposed to be the closest thing we have to magic
and didn't we laugh when the beautiful assistant disappeared?
We did not pity her,
it was not her choice, but we still cheered.
Then you offered those three words on a silver platter,
as if we could feast on immortality—
as if the star from which our souls were first intertwined
would hold our dark love for infinity because that's what the cosmos were meant to do.
But you forgot about supernovas
I believe you forgot that the hydrogen, the helium, the oxygen, the nitrogen—
the chemicals that created the universe
did not create the never-ending film in your head
where the villain is me, but the plot said we had to fall in love.
And isn't it so easy to say it?
Isn't it *too* easy to fall back?
I became the villain because only then would I be immune to your love.
I didn't want to be the damsel in distress you liked to stroke into a state of un-confidence
so that you wouldn't have to climb the tower but wait until I fell down with my walls.
You convinced me that I should celebrate the scars the broken bricks left on my flesh when I crashed.
I believed you.
And you might even be right.

The gravitational pull pulled us back,
that is, of course, Newton's Third Law, and who are we to renounce science?
Light bends around masses, that's why the black hole we live in seems so bright right outside the horizon.

oh.
Did you not notice when our star was destroyed?

You said the force you felt for me never stopped.
I lied and said the same.
Light is fading from my eyes anyway.
And even though it hurts,
those three words are sort of nice to hear
when my coffin is sealed with burnt satin.
Because even after all of this,
even though you say you love me,
you ripped up the flowers on my grave
and refused to kiss me awake from my curse

but you called *this* a second chance.

A Pen & the Classics

What hath I to make amends of grievous care and sin?
Should the Lords of Literature indoctrinate my very pen?
Alas, there be but tombstones to consolidate my fears.
A crown awaits,
and so, the crowd *leers.*

My other lifetimes—
you ought to remember, my dear—
make themselves known in the reflection of glass stains.
He/she/they shed not a tear,
for they know I discredit my luck for the sake of pain.

The skeletons have thus left the closet,
proudly displaying their ridicules of Death,
but bones turn to dust and to Hell, they deposit,
only the ghosts in White Tower contain breath.

Stonewalls should make me beg, and scream, and cry
for I know my past executions over a little white lie—
for love, for jealousy, for the easiness of it all—
be but cures for the medieval anger anchoring my fall.

Thou of immortal pretense and beauty affair
know not of the heart and its pure nightmare.
For God hath broken my flesh upon the altar of morality
as, of course, a proper informality.

These words have come before,
and not a moment too soon.
A life everlasting—
words of impending doom.

- A writer from another time

Haunted

Your nails still dig into my skin sometimes.

I know we're thousands of miles away from each other
and yet
I woke up with three scratch marks on my back
Today. Of course.

I almost thought I had a new scar,
but the blood was dried.
And, upon closer inspection,
the arrowhead was just a knife.

As I am God's witness
(we both know I'm not),
I would have to say I miss you,
but that tastes so bitter on my already-bitten lips
that I cannot tell if it's the truth.

What I can admit,
after I scoured through my closet of bones and dead dreams
just to find shredded paper,
is that there is still ink bleeding out of those shreds,
but I will never tell you that.

Saudade—

Koi No Yokan—

Forelsket— Kilig–

–

Kara sevde—

L'esprit de escalier—

Razbliuto—

La douleurexquise—

Onsra—

Because "love" never did us justice.

If the stars do watch us,
if they know our story,
I am sure they twinkle in the night
to scream at us,
to get us to look up and *see*,
see light,
see each other.

What's the difference, again?

Yet, the moon encircles us in our mutual hatred
and keeps guard against the sun.
We burned ourselves already,
now the Flood has begun.
The part of my heart that is weak,
Soft as you'd like to say, wants—
No—
Needs
to say so many things to you:
Thank you for throwing me to the wolves,
they were much more friendly than I anticipated.
Thank you for pushing me into the waves,
they did, in fact, carry me right back to the sand.
Thank you for shoving me off the cliff,
the fall from grace showed me what freedom is.

An apology is raging in my bloodstream,
A tsunami is quite literally occurring in my veins,
But that would require having to face you
and whatever of *this* that remains.

It is so much easier to let the hatred boil
even though it has already simmered out,
even though there was never any hate there,
just a volcanic eruption that was bound to come about.
Not from you, not really. Just everything inside.
I had never known anything. Except what to hide.

I had never been loved,
and it is so frightening.
Now I understand why they have run away,
I just never thought that *I* would feel that way.
Nor did I think I would ever inflict that pain on another
person.

So, yes, there is a sorry on my lips,
but there's now a cage over my heart,
because, well,
you know what you did.

A Rose of Ruthlessness

Last time
You were the one that reeked of all things dangerous:
the stench of a blunt wafting straight through to my soul,
the permanent ink that stained your skin bled into my veins,
the utterly defiant gleam in your eyes that make me drunk off
  your freedom,

it was You.

You got out a switchblade in the garden,
and I didn't even hesitate to become wild.
In fact,
I think I leaned into the blade.
I wanted to be cut off from the ground.
I wanted to fly with the wind.
I wanted to be like you.
I wanted to be *with* you.

But you did not cut the stem.
You cut off my thorns
because I was a colorblind rose who could only see my
  reflection in the mud.
You knew I wasn't a daffodil,
yet, you tried so hard to keep my vision alive,

and I didn't even know it.
The garden has been unattended for a year now.
The gate is rusted, breaking off its hinges,
vines of malice and spite and pure, unadulterated *rage*
encircle the heart of everything you made better.
Now the term "dangerous" has taken a new form,
it's true form.

The thorns you cut off are back with a vengeance,
I can't even fool myself into believing my petals are yellow anymore.
The red has grown stronger,
darker.
There's still some of your blood on my thorns from the last time you came into the garden.

The Venus Fly Trap is to your left and yet, you're not even scared of it,
not scared of a flower with jaws.
The twinge of your fingertips shows me you are scared of a flower that *loves.*
That's why I'm unhinged,
why the garden let itself rot.
I commanded it to.

The delusional daffodil transformed into the ruthless rose.

But I must still be delusional because there is something within the poisonous tendrils of hatred—
that just wants you back,
that wants the gardener to run soft fingers over crumpled petals,
kiss the thorns on my side because that's all they wanted in the first place.

I didn't think I'd ever see you again.

You don't need to uproot me now
but please,
please
don't let me dry out.

"Turn Off Your Emotions, and You'll Be Unbeatable."

The angel and demon who used to rest on either side of my shoulder quit their job long ago.
I think the angel threw down her halo when I let my lungs fill with smoke and bathed in ash so that the embers of that night when you looked at me differently would also burn my skin, to remind me that I'm alive.
A concept I'm so keen on reading about, but my mind keeps burying in the cemetery right outside of the park we just *almost*-ed in.
The angel lost hope in me.
We used to be so close.
She only came back when I was hospitalized because who knew you could suffocate on tears?
She choked, too.
She choked on the rage,
the hatred,
and the darkness that filled every crevice of my soul.
I wish I could continue that friendship, but she keeps a safe distance from me so that I do not spill black ink onto her wings or write her into my seemingly unholy scripture. She didn't report me to God though so that must count for something.

My demon, on the other hand, left when I took a pen and stabbed my own heart repeatedly until the blood and ink became one toxic mess that replicated the story in my head.
When Hell hides the night from you, it's a clear indicator that there's a limit to villains.
So now I'm just a human standing under a neon sign of a girl whose body makes me bite my tongue.

But I can’t go inside because I’m dangerous but not stupid, and one-dollar bills are better spent on a feeling that will last.

There's a letter you keep mentioning, and I fear that my two guards have ripped it apart. They recognized your name when you asked for an audience, and their trepidation seemed to confirm that they did, in fact, kill the messenger.

I’ve become enamored with a few more colors than the Red I so fondly and despicably am but only when they are all together and only when they can paint you in a picture I can’t reach.

There's an iron grip on my wrist and a viper who likes to encircle my waist. I do not know if she will attack you or bite me. I think only your comments that come so fleetingly will determine her wrath and target.

I wonder if I put cinnamon on my lips if that would make you believe the taste of me is sweet?

The Aftermath

We're different people now.

You say you're still in love, but that girl is gone. Now there's a self-aware demon and her claws are out. Did you not see the three scratches that are on your back from the last time you tried to love me? You thought you were pulling a human out of a glass shell, but it seems, my dear, you tugged darkness out of flesh. I'm sorry you thought there was something sweeter there. I'll be honest, I still wear my halo around my neck, even though it's broken and the gold is rusting from the hellish heat inside my throat— the scream of fire threatening to burn whatever of this we have to the ground. I don't even miss the white feathers you'd like to stroke every Friday night, but I do miss the way we used to talk about heaven. We'd sit on a bed that was adrift in space, and it was as if we were creating our own little universe outside the laws of time, and there was no consequence from being different than the societal roles we were cast in. I hadn't fallen from grace just yet, but I had fallen for you.

But then the Devil whispered all my fears, and I never realized how dangerous light could be. Hell burned up the human but gave me a new soul. I still remember how to look into your eyes, but I'm afraid these black wings will scare you.

Will you still be in love when you see what I've turned into?

A Lost Publication

You were in so many pages in my story that it's hard for me to separate the fact that you were only a chapter in the book.
We were both the broken princesses who turned into villains but regardless of the entire kingdom that was against us, we had each other.
But we were not villains, only victims. And we were not princesses, only girls.
Our love was strong enough to break any curse, but I forgot that we were the ones who cursed ourselves.

Ripped Scriptures

we were gods
planning our plots for the world,
but it's hard to stay gods
when the world wants to burn
- sometimes even i forget my own narrative

Excluded from the Warning Label

Have you ever considered that Love may be the reason for the evils of the world?

But Love is good, you say?

Love is neither good nor evil, it is but the strongest force of nature, which causes the creatures of the earth to act in any way that will secure their heart's desire.

So yes, Love may be the reason you sacrifice yourself.

But it can also be the reason you sacrifice everyone else's lives as well.

"You don't understand,
Love made me do it."

The Worst Thing I've Ever Done

I ripped off the flesh on my palms you would accidentally brush.
I edited my papers so that the remains of your story became blotches of ink
(I even sent them to someone else, but, somehow, she figured out she was the witch and not the princess I wanted).
I stopped romanticizing sunsets over green hills because summer became a simple season.

The farmers' market we never went to but, all the same, belonged to has boarded up.
The fruit now contain pesticides, and the flowers have wilted.
But there is still a part of me that would ingest the toxins and sleep with withered petals if it meant you would walk with me just one more time so I can explain why I fell in love with you in a way like a cloud slipping into the sky instead of the way I did it before—
like a tidal wave crashing into the shore and all you wanted was to dip your toe into the water,
but I ruined the quintessential beach experience,
and I'm so sorry for making you afraid of the ocean.

I didn't realize it the last time I wrote you, but I think I knew it was always on the edge of my vocal cords, threatening to scream it to the world, but you wanted me to whisper, and I just am not capable of hiding in shadows when this feeling is light—
it doesn't belong in the dark, darling.

God,
there's a stellar evolution paradigm, and I should be paying attention to the transition of time, but the only thing I care

about is how we portrayed The Chaos Theory, but we ended up being fractals and
fuck, why?

I thought I was on the Ship of Dreams and you were swimming along next to me with a *midori* tail that gleamed in the moonlight.
But now I can see that you were always a crew member following orders, and I was a siren who had succumbed to my very own tricks. I can only sing The Song of Sorrow and wish upon a childish star that you are swaying to the melody.

But you're not, I would know. I would be able to feel the ricochet in the waves and the echo in the ripple of the universe that supposedly gives second chances.

So here I am, hiding behind the glacier as you steer onward into the chilling future because you made me promise I'd let you sink but that doesn't mean I won't cry in retribution for not being able to say "I love you" for the sake of a goodbye.

Captum Inter et Lux in Tenebris

Is it too much to ask for a light at the end of the tunnel? All I see is darkness, and we've become accustomed to each other's presence, although I fear the darkness is still not entirely comfortable with me here.
It doesn't want me either.
Just like the rest of them.

Then, I guess my question shouldn't be for a light at the end of the tunnel because I don't know if something so blinding would take me as it did so many suburban moms and housewives. I think I have the genetic makeup to fit in, but there is something so distinct about the blue embers in my eyes that are constantly on the verge of setting my iris aflame. It unnerves them. They are used to sunshine and not of unadulterated fire, but they are forgetting what the sun is made of.

So, maybe the light would take me?

The darkness has not kicked me out just yet though. It may be close to it, but it still lets me wander. I always wanted to walk in darkness. Don't tell anyone that, though. I thought the idea was so romantic. I thought if I could escape the confines of a society built by white picket fences and an underground opioid ring, then there would be this mini version of outer space that would show up in my closet and I could dance among the stars.

But that didn't happen. My closet is still full of hand-me-downs and ripped up memories that I am too ashamed to display but too scared to throw away.

A marked-up rivet tied on a silver string hangs in there.

I thought I had thrown it away when I chopped off my hair and vowed to disguise my face under a mask of eyeshadow and social conventions. I had re-invented myself with the help of Aphrodite, and I think Athena has deserted me in the wake of tears I have shed for the past.

I ignore people who open clams up in an attempt to gift me with pearls because I don't want to be another prize. Yet, that never stops them from going back into the sea to destroy natural beings just so they can have an excuse to get close to me.

I would drown if a siren asked me to. She would not even need to sing. I'd happily let her take my face in between her hands, lean into the bite she calls a kiss, and let her do with me as she pleased. To die, I imagine, would be a mercy since it would prevent ignorant minds from believing they could ever say to me "you're mine."

We'll see where this tunnel leaves me.
I'd say "leads," but I don't expect you'll be there at the end.

A Dark Reminder

I kept chasing after sun rays and freckles on faces that were sun-kissed because I equivocated love to light, but it's just how you become blind.
I fit the description of the naiveté. The doe eyes, the bottom lip that juts out to trick you into a kiss, the pale complexion makeup artists mistake for porcelain so they can paint the doll they never had when they were younger.
I pretend that the color black is a superpower that I can wear and all of society's expectations of me will disappear, but when your summer comes, I'm forced to put the jacket away or else I'll get burned by the truth and sweat out the fake persona I built.

But the Sun and I are not friends.
He knows that I have been moon-kissed since a celestial night bathed me in stardust and an afterlife delight.
I never told him about the kiss, but he must have seen the echo of a star's shadow in my eyes that wasn't his and set the timer on his supernovae.
I wake up each morning graced with a lunar intensity that pushes me back to bed because I am meant to dream with her;
I am not for daylight.
I think her biggest vex is that I was raised in the doorway of a Catholic household and cannot shake off the demons a priest's philosophy gave me.
If I squint, I can still see the scars from the shattering of a crystalline case of holy water, and I don't know if I was hurt from the glass or the purity
If it was up to her, we would be lying in a field from an afternoon picnic that went on far too long, and yet it was too

short all the same. If you're still scared, I know she would hide us in a crater from the light.
The Dark Side of the Moon could be the heaven we almost knew. That is, if you had said that you loved me too.
That's why I keep going back to the Sun. The light shows me that some dreams, however enchanting like the curve of your jaw or the petal fingertips that used to tap at my lower back, were never meant for the light of day.

And I still need to be reminded of that.

May Wildfires

we said we loved summer
and the transition from green grass to gold,
but you showed me a burnt hillside,
and i think we were meant to meet in a different season

- call me when we bloom again

Self-Redemption

Fears hit you in a different way.

The fear of failure makes you freeze.
You stop yourself from jumping off a cliff because you are unsure if you can swim in murky waters.
The mermaids underneath transform into demons and sharks circle the single drop of blood you spilled.
So, you do not jump based off a vision you never saw.
The mermaids call out, but you refuse to sing.
Thus, life never becomes anything.

The fear of life lost makes you hide.
You have not met Death, but you act as though the kind being is your nemesis.
The blinds on your windows have transformed into bars, and the same amount of locks on your doors matches the number you have on your heart.
You claim the world is cruel, but it was you who made your prison cell.
The birds chirp, flowers grow, and the sky is a beautiful blue,
but you'd never know because you only believe in the world you once knew.

The fear of love makes you hurt.
You throw around hearts like you throw around playthings from your childhood,
and you break them just as quickly as you did back then too.
You see something foreign in a potential lover's eyes, and you don't just abandon ship.
You destroy the ship and ensure it sinks to the bottom of the ocean.

You lie with skeletons on the ocean floor that you mistake for lost treasure,
and you make sure to break their bones too, just for good measure.

It is the fear of being yourself which seems to be the most frightening.
Watchful eyes of all-knowing figures seem to follow every footstep.
You run and run and run, but you don't know if you are running from Them or yourself.
Escape is never an option because no thriller ever ended quietly.
It is the only fear that every individual is forced to face one day.

I seldom do but conquering fears are sometimes the only way to keep on living.

The Sword in the Closet

"You have something of mine," I said, lifting my sword as I prepared for battle.

You laughed and picked it up as if it was an apple you planned to take a bite out of. "This oldthing?"

Nodding feverishly, my hand reached forward only for my fingertips to meet air. "You have no use for it now. It's mine. You have to give it back."

Your smirk only grew. "But you gave it to me."

"No, you stole it from me!"

"Same thing." You yawned, bored of the bickering.

Filled with fury, I placed my blade at your neck and demanded for you to give me my rightful possession. It was *so close.*

You laughed. The sword should have made a cut, but none appeared. You laughed some more as you traced a finger over it. "You'll just lose itagain."

That was true.

"If not for me, it would be wrongly given to someone else."

"Or the right one."

You smirked. "Then maybe you should have considered that before you gave it away so freely."

I lowered my sword. You were right. I looked at it closer. It was pathetically pulsing, still carrying on even through the pain. My heart had been damaged, but I could see the healing process begin in the few seconds it was out of your palm.

That had to mean something.
And so,
I kept fighting.

We Have Different Endings

Most of the poetry in this book is written about you, did you know?

There was a time when the ink of every pen bled all over each paper I had.
Then I met you and the ink made a few words of something readable.
I didn't even know that I was writing about you.
The ink that bled over paper soon circulated in my heart.

They tell me to chase after my dreams, but I know that I cannot chase you.
Although it feels like my pen drew the words that line your skin,
I didn't create you, you created yourself from the pages of a different book.
Though you only let me read a few chapters, you are my favorite story.

I have never been scared to read a book before.

I was told I was emotionally immature before being thrust into the adult world,
A world where love and lust seem to be regarded as the same thing.
Every childhood story tells you of a happily ever after.
I know that is not the ending to our story.

In spite of fantasy ruining our reality, in spite of a "true love's kiss" that never was,

There was a beautiful princess who taught a poor writer how to believe.
The only villains in our story are ourselves, and I wouldn't want it any other way.
But if you ever think back on that dream from once upon another time—

Please read our story again.

The Story

It's a rare and fleeting feeling now that I suspect comes with the aggrievance of time.
Time, the age-old killer,
the god we pray to for mercy—
I just need a little more *TIME*—
to enact redemption.

I've been finding dust over the things I used to love, even the notebooks of love letters I know I burned for when rushed fevered notes were all I was capable of writing.

Slick and pale blue,
an empty room seems more befitting of myself than a trinket treasure trove to a girl I can no longer reflect onto a scratched-up mirror.

Time killed her, did you know? I am sure he'll kill me too some time, but I know he is a little more content now that the hidden kiss on the corner of my mouth is not so hidden anymore.

To be fair, I put up a great fight against Time. Which is most likely the reason for my delay in every way.
And is why he was forced to age me with a broken heart.

It was like a spell had been broken, but I had not been kissed awake by any princess, rather I was roughly shoved off the bed and promptly thrown into battle with a letter opener as my only weapon against an enemy much stronger than I could ever imagine.

Defeat was inevitable. You never win your first fight. But I could have gotten off the ground.

Instead, I stayed still in a newly formed graveyard of childhood memories. The toys I played with were scattered around, cotton fluff pillowing out of their stomachs from the blow of battle. There were colors too that had meant so much as they were a whisper of the sun's special goodbye— the pink and the blue— the hues that had warmed me enough to keep me smiling on a cold, moon-full night— were sinking into the ground, dripping in distaste for me
And, of course,
in retreat.

There was my old pen pal to my left, but it was my blood on the notes.
She was on the other side.

The thing you need to know most ardently about my star-fled afflictions is how concretely and volcanically stubborn I can be. That's the only way this story will make sense.

You see, I lay on blood-soaked grass for perhaps eons as I refused to admit that I had not lost the war but myself.

The constellations took on new meanings
(but you know they would never change their stories)
and the waves crashed for retribution.

But I did not wish on stars for I could not allow myself even the slight silver wink of weakness. I did not pick up a seashell to talk to the ocean because I wanted to become dangerous on my own.

It was not until a thorn-studded rose, (that was painted in the massacre of my own soul), grew around my wrist that I knew I had to move on.

I was a daffodil once.
At some level in the multiple universes in my head, I'd like to believe a daffodil is still there. But the crimson caress of all things dark was a permanent stain on my skin, and, frankly,
I was tired of running away.

Red became a staple, and it seemed the rest of the world knew it meant all things in correlation withme.
A leather jacket was my armor, and this time, I had a much more powerful weapon once I broke the wand of the witch that cursed me.

It was the battle royale and a high seas crusade. The sirens mistook me for them, and, honestly,
I was pleased.
There were victims and heroes and I was a distressed damsel of a villain, but Time knew what he was doing, and I'd like to believe he's the only one I can trust.

Sometimes I still see that kingdom from which I once ruled. The castle is in the ruins of ghosts' wake and the enchanted forest has been knocked down for some capitalistic endeavor.
But there does still seem to be a strange charm and even stranger sense of *maybe*.

The ones I had the most trouble forgiving were that of the constellations who refused to change their stories for me when all I wanted was a star that I could identify with.

So, in spite of navigating rough seas and depths of despair, I did not look up into my eternal night, rather I memorized the currents and counted the number of ripples in the ocean.
The sea and I were equals now
(and apparently, we always were)
The constellations were dropping stardust on me in an effort to make peace, but I brushed it off into the waves to take and that's how you met me.

I knew you were there, by the ship, watching and waiting, but you were careful and cautious— it's common sense not to trust a knight-turned-pirate.

It was little things at first.
A splash there,
A knock here,
A melody in the wind that seemed to echo everywhere
I think it was a test, and I was a little busy chasing after a map of myths while simultaneously keeping a weather eye on the horizon (just in case my old pen pal wasn't done writing my ending)

There's a reason mermaids are so dangerous. Sure, the Aphrodite-blessed features and the ambrosia-infused voice are enough to make any living creature melt, but it was the kindness that sunk me.

It is ironically irrelevant to the functions of my character,
I had known soft gestures once
(princesses have *gentle* curves),
and I guess I didn't realize I was losing weight
when I was purposefully starving myself of affection.

So, when your fingerprints left accidental bruises on my sea-stained skin as you pulled me up to sanded memories, a satin and silked sunset weaved its way behindyou.
It outlined the wreckage of my vendetta vessel,
It shed light on the tail of a passenger who stowed away in my mind,
It dried off the scars I thought would fade only after death,
Yet the most important thing it did was remind me I was, in fact, incapable of drowning on the land that anchored me to every fallen stone of killers/thrillers, and, I guess,
happy endings.

I admit,
it took me a moment to register that I had done this to myself, and if it hadn't been for you, I would not have come out of the wreck unscathed.
Yes, there are jagged lines of neon regret and plum betrayal that are *oh so visible* for our world to see but they are old wounds that I have been clawing at,
ripping apart the spiderweb cracked scabs,
because even though my body is healing, my heart is still broken and wants revenge for taking away the me that looked directly at the sun in spite of all the warnings because I thought he needed a friend—

fine, honesty hour it is:
I am *upset* I never had a moment to say goodbye before the tower crumbled.
I am *angry* that I did not get to savor tokens of the past like the bolt on a silver string (which had been my finest necklace handcrafted by a maiden before she burned herself at the stake).

I am *ashamed* that I mistook sweet nothings for superficial spells by a witch who only wanted to show me a different narrative. I owe her so many apologies.
I am *distraught* that frogs hopped after me, leaned into my throne, and tried to force me to play a part I have never been right for. All I could do was turn my head so that they got my cheek and not the lips that I wanted to reserve for someone special because,
as brutal as I am,
there's still this strange, stupid, and starry-eyed romantic in me that cannot tolerate anything but True Love. I can, of course, relate to another creature who is as cursed as me but to Love? I am so sorry; I am not capable of turning you into a Prince.

In my unconscious awakening, I did not even register that my savior, the mermaid with the *midori* tail, had retreated into safe waters. I should have told her I loved her from the moment I first heard her knock against the stern of the ship of dreams. There is one last look of something I could mistake for hatred if she had not stopped me from drowning myself. Her eyes are alight with electric fury, eyebrows furrowed in disbelief, and the fuchsia flush on her face tells me we *almost*-ed and maybe that's why she'll never forgive me.
Nevertheless, the ocean holds so many secret sins, so she sinks her head underwater because it is less painful to go under the waves than be knocked back by the weight of truth.

By now, you've realized Time is an allegory for growing up. In front of me is the red and golden pebbled pathway to whatever lies next and—

How foolish I have been

to only now uncover the fact
that no story
ever
really
ends

Thank you for reading!

Please consider leaving a review to help other readers find this work.

Discover more titles from other GenZ authors at Genzpublishing.org.

About the Author

I am an individual who got a tattoo on a whim without really thinking about *what* I wanted staining my skin forever, but I salvage the recklessness that rests on my hip. I am the girl who falls so hard in love that the scattered and sap-filled poetry in my journal has only ever been over three different people. I am the supervillain turned anti-hero because people taught me there were worse things than myself. I am the kid who is struggling to understand adulthood because I have only ever known the marble stepping-stones that lead up to college but fear the drop off next to Icarus. I am the pirate who throws lyrics in a bottle and sends them across the sea, hoping a siren can perform them with me. I am the person who pecked the cheek of a boy, kissed the lips of a girl, but then lied on a werewolf's chest. I am the time traveler who loves to visit the future despite the pull from the '80s retro aesthetic. I am the spirit that haunts my own self because the echoes of past lives from my darkest days in a Hell called high school ring louder and louder as I tend to sing along to my own misery. I am an admirer of the stars and all the stories that lie within the infinite chasm of all of time and space. I am a biker without a motorcycle but have the leather jacket and red lipstick to match, chasing after an open road that not even God could see the end to. I am the artist without art except for the occasional makeup palette to entice the subject in my poetry. I am the Knight in Shining Armor who took pride in killing dragons until I realized the creatures were just as scared as I was. I am the architect who is designing a plan lined with gold edges that can only be built by myself. I am the asshole who speaks in riddles and glares when I cannot comprehend what society is asking me to be. I am the explorer who is still climbing mountains and mountains and even more mountains inside my head as I push myself to be the person I need to be, forever seeking *that* person. I am a rebel with a few causes to spare: for the world, for the people I love, but really, for myself. As you might have guessed, I am a writer who scrapes her body with every punch of a pen so that I may bleed the black ink that circulates my veins. Yet, the most significant thing you need to know about me is that I am K.G.Ginley.

About the Publisher

GenZ Publishing emphasizes new, emerging, young, and underrepresented authors. We're an indie publisher that focuses on mentoring authors through each step of the publishing process and beyond: editing, writing sequels, cover design, marketing, PR, and even getting agented for future works. We love to see our authors succeed both with the books they publish with us and with their other publications. That's why we call it the "GenZ Family."

For more information, visit Genzpublishing.org or contact us at info@genzpublishing.org. Connect with us on Instagram, Facebook, Twitter, and LinkedIn for our latest news and releases.

CPSIA information can be obtained
at www.ICGtesting.com
Printed in the USA
JSHW031701130521
14665JS00002B/123

9 781952 919343